The Curse

I Talk You Talk Press

CONTENTS

INTRODUCTION

Billy and Joey are art thieves. They steal expensive paintings from art galleries, old castles and homes. Then, they sell the paintings to buyers. They make a lot of money doing this.

Billy is older than Joey. He is a very clever art thief and he enjoys stealing paintings. The police can never catch him.

Joey is a little different. He feels bad when he steals paintings. But he likes Billy very much. Billy is like an older brother to Joey, and he wants to be with Billy all the time. Also, he likes the money he gets for stealing paintings. He buys his mother many things with the money. His mother thinks he has a good job in a bank. She doesn't know he is a thief. Billy doesn't buy his mother anything. He likes gambling and fast cars.

Billy and Joey are professionals. They know a lot about museum and home security. They have stolen paintings from museums in the daytime, and at night.

They have many different ways of stealing paintings. Sometimes, when they steal paintings in the daytime, Joey wears a hat and a fake beard and walks into a museum. Then, he takes the painting off the wall and runs out of the museum. The security guards chase him, but he is so fast that they never catch him. Joey runs to Billy who is waiting in the getaway car, and then they escape.

Sometimes, when they want to steal a painting, Billy and Joey pretend to be repair or maintenance workers. When a museum is having repairs, they go to the museum wearing workmen's clothes. Then, they break the security camera system and take the paintings.

Once, Joey got a job as a night time security guard in a museum.

He left the door open and fell asleep. Billy came in and took the painting. Joey got fired from his job because he fell asleep, but no one knew he was one of the thieves.

Now, Billy and Joey are in a meeting with Mr Sweeney, a very rich art collector. Mr Sweeney is a bad man. He often asks Billy and Joey to steal paintings for him and his friends.

CHAPTER ONE

Billy and Joey are sitting in Mr Sweeney's office. The office is on the top floor of a very tall building in the centre of London.

Mr Sweeney lights a cigarette and says, "I have a new job for you. A difficult job."

"A difficult job? Good. I like a challenge," says Billy. "What is it?"

"It is more difficult than any other job," says Mr Sweeney. "I want you to get the painting called *The Girl in the Blue Dress*."

Billy and Joey look at Mr Sweeney. Then they look at each other. They are very shocked.

After about a minute, Joey speaks.

"*The Girl in the Blue Dress?*" he says quietly. "In Boglow Castle?"

"Yes. *The Girl in the Blue Dress*, by the famous artist Décor," says Mr Sweeney. He walks over to the office window and looks down on the city of London. It is raining and the clouds are very dark.

Billy and Joey look at each other again nervously.

"As you know, there is a famous story about the painting. It was painted in 1850. The young girl in the painting was the daughter of Lord Boglow II, the owner and resident of the castle at that time. She loved the castle and didn't like to leave. She especially liked her room. She used to cry when her mother and father tried to take her on trips away from the castle.

"When she was nine, Décor painted her portrait. A few weeks later, she died of an illness. Her father, Lord Boglow II, was very upset. He put the painting in his daughter's bedroom and spent many hours every day sitting on her bed and looking at the painting. Before

Décor died, someone said to him, 'You have painted many pictures. Which is your favourite?' Décor answered, *'The Girl in the Blue Dress.'* After that, many people wanted to see the painting, and it became very famous. A few years later, a thief stole the painting. Soon after he stole it, he died mysteriously. It's one of Décor's most famous works, and it has been stolen four times."

"And every time someone steals it, something bad happens, and the thief dies mysteriously," says Joey. "The painting is cursed."

"Ah, the curse! Yes!" says Mr Sweeney. He laughs and takes a sip of whisky. "You don't believe that story, do you?"

"I don't," says Billy. "I don't believe in curses."

"I don't believe it either," says Mr Sweeney. "How about you, Joey?"

Joey takes a long drink from his glass of whisky.

"I believe it," he says quietly. "It has been stolen four times. And every time, the thief has died. That is not a coincidence," says Joey. "There is something mysterious about the painting."

"Do you believe in Santa Claus, too?" asks Billy.

"Do you believe in angels and fairies?" asks Mr Sweeney.

Mr Sweeney and Billy laugh.

"Joey, you are like a child!" says Mr Sweeney.

Joey scowls and looks out of the window. Mr Sweeney and Billy often make jokes about him, because he is young. He is twenty-five, but Billy is forty-five, and Mr Sweeney is sixty. Billy sometimes calls him Baby Joey. Joey really does not like that name.

"OK, let's forget about the fairy story. Let's talk about the important thing. The money," says Billy. "Mr Sweeney, how much will you pay us?"

"Well, because the painting is by Décor, and because people believe there is a curse, it's very expensive. So, I will pay you a million pounds," says Mr Sweeney.

Billy and Joey look at each other.

"A-a-a-a…a million pounds?" whispers Billy.

When Billy and Joey steal paintings, they usually get twenty or thirty thousand pounds. They have never got a millions pounds for stealing a painting.

"Yes, a million," says Mr Sweeney. "Can you do it?"

Billy nods his head. "Yes, Mr Sweeney. Of course we can. Of course we can."

"I don't know…" says Joey. A million pounds is a lot of money. He wants the money. But he is very worried about the curse.

Billy kicks him. "Of course we can do it! Of course!" says Billy. "Can't we Joey?"

Joey looks at Billy. Billy kicks him again.

"Yes, we can do it," says Joey quietly.

"Good," says Mr Sweeney. "I will rent a flat for you in Manchester, ten miles away from the castle. You can stay there while you plan the theft. When you get the painting, take it back to the flat and then call me. I will come and get it, and I will pay you in cash."

"OK," says Billy.

"So, are you ready?" asks Mr Sweeney.

"Yes, we are!" says Billy.

Joey nods his head. He is not so sure. He is worried about the curse.

"Go home and pack your bags. I will arrange a car for you. You will drive up to Manchester tomorrow," says Mr Sweeney.

Billy and Joey thank Mr Sweeney and leave his office.

They walk out into the busy street. The autumn wind is cold, and it is still raining.

"This is a great job!" says Billy. "After this job, I'm going to have a rest for a few years. I'm going to take my half of the million pounds and go to a tropical island and relax. Life is great!"

"Yes, it is," says Joey quietly.

"Hey, Baby Joey! What's wrong? Are you still worried about the curse? You really are a baby, aren't you!" says Billy, laughing.

"No, I'm not," says Joey. He lights a cigarette and turns away from Billy. "I'm fine, I'm fine."

Billy and Joey go to bed early that night, but Joey cannot sleep. He has a bad feeling about this job. A very bad feeling…

CHAPTER TWO

Billy and Joey arrive in Manchester and go to the flat. It is in a nice area of the city and has wonderful views, but Billy and Joey have no time to enjoy them. They have a very important job to do. They must plan the theft of the painting.

They find the website of the castle and print out maps and tourist pamphlets. They also check the area on Google Earth.

The owners of the castle are Lord and Lady Boglow. Lord Boglow VI is the great-great-grandson of Lord Boglow II, the girl's father. Lord Boglow VI and his wife, Lady Boglow, live in one part of the castle. The rest of the castle is open to the public. Visitors can walk around the gardens, and there are guided tours around public areas of the castle. Many tourists visit the castle every year because they want to see the famous Décor painting.

Now, Billy and Joey are sitting in the living room in the flat. They are thinking about the best way to steal the painting.

"Should we take the painting in the daytime, or at night?" asks Joey.

"I don't know. We have to visit the castle first and check the security," says Billy. "But I don't think security will be very tight. The curse of the painting is very famous, so most art thieves don't want to steal the painting. When a thief steals the painting, bad things happen. Everyone knows that. So, now, no one tries to steal the painting. I think this will be a very easy job."

"I see," says Joey. He is still very nervous. "Do you think we will be safe?"

"Joey! Nothing bad will happen! I promise! I'm like an older brother to you, Joey. I will protect you! I promise!" says Billy. "Don't you trust me Joey?"

"Of course I trust you Billy," says Joey. "Of course I trust you."

Later that night, they drink and play cards, but Joey cannot concentrate. All he thinks about is the curse.

CHAPTER THREE

The next morning, Billy and Joey get up early and plan their day. They will go to the castle to check the security situation. There will be security cameras in the castle, so they have to wear a disguise. Billy wears a grey suit, glasses and a fake beard. Joey wears casual clothes, a baseball cap and sunglasses.

They look at each other.

"Hey, Billy, you look like an art professor!" says Joey.

"And you look like an art student!" says Billy.

Joey laughs. "At least we don't look like Billy and Joey, the art thieves!"

Billy and Joey go to the castle at 9:00am. It is raining, and dark clouds cover the sky. The castle is in the middle of a large forest with very tall trees. There is a big iron gate and a small hut next to the gate. A security guard is sitting in the hut.

They drive up to the gate and the security guard smiles at them as they pass through the gate and drive to the car park.

Billy parks the car and casually looks around the car park for security cameras. He cannot see any. Joey looks up at the castle. It looks cold and unwelcoming in the rain.

"This is going to be an easy job, Joey. An easy job," says Billy.

A large tour bus comes into the car park, and many people get off the bus.

"Come on, let's go into the castle with this tour group," says Billy.

They get out of the car and walk into the house behind the tour group. They buy tickets for a tour at the reception desk, and follow the group of people into the castle.

"Good morning everyone. Welcome to the Boglow Castle tour," says the guide.

"Today, you are going to see some rooms of the castle and the rose gardens. You are also going to see something very special," says the guide. "You are going to see *The Girl in the Blue Dress.*"

Everyone starts talking excitedly. Joey suddenly feels very nervous. Sweat starts to run down his back.

They walk around the castle with the guide. The guide talks about the history of the castle and the Boglow family. The castle has many rooms, and there are expensive antiques everywhere. The Boglow family is one of Britain's richest families. While the guide is talking, Billy and Joey look around for security cameras and exits.

They go up to the second floor, and the guide takes them into a large bedroom.

"Ladies and gentleman, this is it! This is the girl's bedroom. And this is the painting," says the guide. "*The Girl in the Blue Dress.*"

Everyone looks at the painting. In the painting is a young girl, wearing a blue dress.

"This painting is very famous," says the guide. "It is one of Décor's most important paintings. It also has a curse. The young girl in the painting lived here. She loved Boglow Castle, and she loved living here. But she died very young."

Everyone in the group is listening very carefully.

"This room was her bedroom," says the guide. "It was her favourite room in the house. So her family put the painting here. That is her bed and over there is her dressing table." The guide pointed to the small bed and dressing table. Then, he pointed to a large box on the floor. "And that is her toy box. It is empty because the toys are on the floor and on the bed. She always enjoyed playing with her toys."

Joey feels very cold. He looks at the girl in the painting. She has a gentle smile and seems to be looking directly at him. He starts to sweat even more.

"Tell us the story about the thieves," says a woman in the group.

"Well, this was Décor's favourite painting, so it became very expensive. In 1860, a man broke into the castle and stole the painting from this room. The day after he stole the painting, he died suddenly."

"How did he die?" asks the woman.

"We don't know," says the guide. "He was found dead in his bed. It's still a mystery. After that, many people were frightened. They said 'The painting has a curse!' So for a long time, no one tried to steal it. Then, 100 years later, in 1960, another man tried to steal it. He took it off the wall and ran down the stairs. Near the entrance, he tripped and fell through a glass window. Of course, he died instantly," says the guide.

"Then, about ten years later, a group of thieves stole the painting. They escaped and took the painting to London. A few days later, they were all killed in a fire. After that, the castle got a better security system and it was safe until 1995. Then, a bad security guard took the painting. A few weeks later, he was at the beach with his friends. He was swimming in the sea, when he suddenly disappeared. He was found a few hours later. He was dead."

"So, no one wants to steal the painting now?" asks a woman in the group.

"No. No one will steal this painting," says the guide. "It has been stolen four times. Every time, the thief died. So now, art thieves are very afraid of the curse. They know that if they steal the painting, they will die. So I think this painting is very safe."

"Why does the painting have a curse?" asks the woman.

"People say it is because the girl loved living here so much. She didn't want to die. She wanted to live here for a long time. But she couldn't," says the guide. "So, her spirit gets angry when people try to take her away from here."

Joey starts to feel sick. He doesn't want to do this job.

There are so many other expensive paintings in the world. Why can't we get a different painting? he thinks.

The tour moves to a different room. Joey looks around, but he cannot concentrate. He is frightened. He looks at Billy.

Billy is so calm, he thinks. *He doesn't believe in the curse. I want to be strong like Billy. Why can't I be strong like Billy?*

CHAPTER FOUR

Later that night, Billy and Joey buy some fish and chips and beer. They go back to the flat and sit at the kitchen table.

"This is going to be a very easy job," says Billy. "Thanks to the curse, no one wants to steal the painting. So security is not so tight."

Joey drinks his beer.

"But I think it is strange. It has been stolen four times. And every time the thieves died!" says Joey.

"Are you still worried about the curse?" says Billy. "Joey, you really are a baby. There is no curse. The thieves died in accidents. That's all."

Billy takes a drink from his beer bottle.

"This is your job, Joey. You have to think like a professional. Professionals don't worry about children's stories. OK?"

"OK," says Joey quietly. "OK."

"Good. Now, let's talk business," says Billy, lighting a cigarette. "There is a security camera at the entrance, one on the stairs, and one outside the girl's room. There are no cameras in the room. How many security guards did you see?"

"I saw one at the gate, and two walking around the house and gardens. They didn't have guard dogs or weapons," says Joey.

"Good," says Billy. "Now, here is the plan. We cannot steal the painting in the daytime. The painting is on the second floor. It will take a long time to run down the stairs and into the car park. The security guard will call the police. And the road from the car park through the forest is very long. The police will wait for us at the end of the road. So, we have to steal it at night."

"How will we do that?" asks Joey.

"It's easy. We go to the castle again in the afternoon. On our way back from the castle today, I saw an old barn next to the forest. We can park the car in the barn. No one will find it," says Billy.

"We will take some strong rope and some tools. We can put them under our coats. The last tour is at 4:00pm. We join the 4:00pm tour. When the tour group leaves the girl's room, I will lie under the bed, and you will get inside the toy box. The house closes at 5:00pm. When night comes, we will carefully take the painting out of the frame. The painting is not so big, so I can put it under my shirt. Then, we open the window and use the rope to escape," says Billy.

"Is there a security alarm on the window?" asks Joey.

"No, there were no wires. I checked," says Billy.

"How about cameras outside?" asks Joey.

"There is a camera, but it points in the opposite direction. There is an entrance on the other side, so the camera faces that," says Billy. "Joey, you should notice things like this. You have to check the cameras and wires. We didn't visit the castle for a fun trip. This is work!"

"Yes, of course," says Joey. He didn't notice the camera and he didn't look at the windows because he was thinking about the curse.

"Then, we run across the front gardens and climb over the wall."

"How will we climb over the wall? It's very high," says Joey.

"We will take some thick rope. You will stand on my shoulders and tie it to a tree on the other side of the wall. Then, we climb over."

"I see," says Joey. "Then what will we do?"

"We will run through the forest to the car, and then drive away. Easy!" says Billy. "In the morning, when the security guards notice that the painting has been stolen, we will already be far away. What do you think?"

Joey thinks about it. It seems like a good plan. And Billy is a professional. He has many years of experience. But he is still worried about the curse…

That night, in bed, Joey tries to sleep. Every time he closes his eyes, he sees the girl's face. Her eyes look angry. He tries to sleep, but he cannot. He lies awake all night, watching the sky as it slowly becomes light.

CHAPTER FIVE

It is 3:00pm.

Billy and Joey drive to the old barn next to the forest. They get out of the car and look around the barn. There is no lock on the large wooden doors, so they walk in.

"Perfect!" says Billy. "There is space for many cars in here!"

Joey looks around. There are some old farm machines at the back of the barn, and there are holes in the roof and walls.

"It's very dark, Billy. Will we be OK tonight?" asks Joey.

"Of course we will! Stop worrying!" says Billy. He gets back into the car and drives it into the barn.

"Come on Joey. Let's go. It will take us around thirty minutes to walk to the castle from here," says Billy.

They walk quickly through the forest until they get to the gate.

"Good afternoon, gentlemen," says the old security guard.

"Good afternoon," say Billy and Joey.

"Have you been walking in the forest?" says the security guard.

"Yes, we have," says Billy. "We enjoy walking and hiking. Can we still enter the castle?"

"Yes, of course. The last tour is at 4:00pm, so if you hurry, you can join it," says the security guard.

"Really?" says Joey. "We must hurry. Thank you very much."

"Enjoy your visit gentlemen," says the guard.

"We will!" says Billy as they walk through the gate.

Billy and Joey go into the castle and buy tickets for the tour. They are lucky. There are around twenty people waiting for the tour. No one will notice when they disappear.

The tour starts. The tour guide is the same man as last time, but he doesn't recognize Billy and Joey because they are wearing different clothes and they have changed their hair colour. Billy has dyed his hair brown, and Joey has dyed his hair blond. They look very different.

The tour guide takes the group up the stairs to the second floor.

"And now, we are going to see the painting *The Girl in the Blue Dress*," says the guide. Joey starts to feel sick. They walk into the room.

"This painting is very famous," says the guide. "It is one of Décor's most important paintings. It also has a curse. The young girl in the painting lived here…"

Some people ask questions, but Joey cannot hear the questions. He is looking at the girl's face. Her face looks different. She looks very sad. Joey looks at Billy. Billy looks normal. He doesn't look nervous.

"OK, let's go to the next room," says the guide.

Everyone walks out of the room. Billy and Joey wait until the last person has left. Then, Billy quickly gets under the bed and Joey jumps in the toy box, quickly puts his gloves on, and pulls the lid over his head. The guide is answering questions from the other people on the tour, so no one notices Billy and Joey disappear.

Joey is very nervous and he cannot breathe very well. Inside the toy box is very dark. He cannot see anything. Around thirty minutes later, he hears the sound of cars and buses leaving the car park.

"Billy!" he whispers.

"Shh!!" says Billy. "Wait!"

Joey holds his breath. The toy box is very dusty. He wants to sneeze. Then, he hears footsteps. It is the security guard on patrol. He holds his nose, but he can't stop. He sneezes. "Acchoo!!"

The footsteps stop, and the guard walks into the room.

From under the bed, Billy can see the guard's feet. The guard walks around the room and stands near the toy box.

Oh no! This is it, thinks Joey. *The guard is going to find me! My mother will be so angry when she finds out about this!*

He closes his eyes and waits for the guard to lift the lid off the box and find him. Then he hears the guard walk out of the room and close the door. *He didn't find me! He didn't find me! I'm so lucky!* thinks

Joey.

The room becomes darker. The castle has closed for the day, and outside, the light is fading. It will soon be night.

After about an hour, he hears Billy's voice.

"Joey! Joey!" whispers Billy from under the bed.

"Billy! Are you OK under the bed?" asks Joey.

"Yes, I am! Are you OK in the toy box?" asks Billy.

"Yes, but I want to go to the toilet," says Joey.

"You can't go to the toilet! Why didn't you go before the tour started?" asks Billy.

"I didn't need to go to the toilet then. But I do now," says Joey.

"You have to be strong!" says Billy. "You are not a child Joey! You are a man! You have to wait!" says Billy.

"Yes Billy," says Joey. He stops talking and waits.

CHAPTER SIX

Every hour, Billy and Joey hear the guard's footsteps outside the room.

They notice that the guard patrols the second floor once every hour.

They wait a little longer. Then, an hour later, they hear the guard again. When the guard has gone, Billy rolls out from under the bed.

"Joey!" he whispers. "It's time!"

Joey lifts up the lid off the toy box and stands up.

"Are you OK?" asks Billy.

Joey stretches. "Yes, I'm OK, but I still need to go to the toilet."

"Just wait a little longer," says Billy. He pulls out the tools from his coat.

"Come on, let's start."

They walk over to the painting. The room is very dark, but there is a little light from the moon outside. Joey looks around the room. There are many shadows in the moonlight. Then he looks at the girl in the painting, and starts to feel frightened again.

"Come on Joey! Stop dreaming! We don't have much time!" says Billy.

The painting frame is on a hook and wire. Billy cuts the wire very easily and takes the painting off the hook. He puts the painting on the floor. Together, Billy and Joey cut the back of the frame. The wood is very thick, so it is very difficult to cut. It takes them a long time. They have to be very careful because they don't want to damage the painting.

"Shh!!" says Billy suddenly.

"What?" whispers Joey.

They hear footsteps outside.

"It's the guard again!" whispers Billy.

Billy and Joey are confused. Has an hour passed already?

The footsteps stop outside the door. Joey starts to sweat. He can feel the cold sweat running down his back. His hands start to shake. Billy watches the door very closely. They wait. Then, after about ten seconds, the footsteps start again, and the guard goes away.

Billy takes a deep breath. "That was scary!" he whispers.

"Has an hour passed?" asks Joey.

"Maybe. This frame is very hard to break," says Billy. "Come on, let's work harder."

They break the frame at last and Billy carefully lifts the painting out of the frame. He rolls it up and puts it under his coat.

"Come on! Get the rope!" says Billy.

Joey pulls the rope out from under his coat.

"What should I tie the rope to?" asks Joey.

Billy and Joey look around the room.

"The dressing-table leg!" says Billy. "That looks strong."

Joey ties the rope to the dressing table leg and goes to the window. Very carefully, he opens the catch on the window. He pushes at the window and it opens slowly.

The cool night air fills the room. Joey looks down from the window and breathes deeply. The second floor is very high. It is a long way down to the ground. He feels sick. He doesn't like high places.

Billy punches Joey's back. "What are you waiting for? Let's go! The guard will be back soon! Start running when you get to the ground. Don't wait for me. I will meet you at the wall. OK?"

"OK, Billy. I'll see you at the wall."

Joey throws the rope down to the ground outside. He hears the rope hit the ground.

"Go!" whispers Billy.

Joey climbs out of the window and slides down the rope in the moonlight. The night is cold, and he can feel the wind on his face. He closes his eyes and climbs down the rope. He lands on the ground and looks around. It is very dark so he cannot see anything.

"I'm coming down!" whispers Billy. "Run!" Billy starts to climb down the rope.

Joey starts to run.

"No Joey! Stop! Stop! You are running the wrong way!" shouts Billy.

Joey looks up at Billy.

"What?" he says.

Suddenly a light comes on.

"Hey you!"

Joey jumps in shock. He looks up. There is the security guard running towards him! Joey has run the wrong way! He has run straight into a security guard on patrol!

He panics.

"Billy! There's a guard! Quick! Run!!" he shouts.

Billy lands on the ground and they start to run across the garden. Lights start to come on in the castle and an alarm starts to ring. They run across the dark grass. The light from the castle helps them to see.

A security guard holding a bright torch is running after them. Security alarms are ringing all around the castle.

They hear a security patrol car driving into the car park.

"The gate is open! Quick!" says Billy.

The night-time security guard at the gate has opened it for the security patrol car to come through.

As they run to the gate, the security guard at the gate tries to stop them, but the guard is an old man, and Billy and Joey are too fast for him. They run through the dark forest.

Through the trees, they see a police car driving very quickly towards the castle car park. They don't stop running until they get to the barn.

They open the barn doors and jump into the car.

"Let's go!" says Billy as he starts the car engine.

They drive very quickly away from the barn and the forest. They drive onto the main road and onto the motorway. They don't stop until they are 50 miles away.

CHAPTER SEVEN

Billy and Joey stop in a service station car park.

"Did anyone see the car?" asks Joey.

"No, they didn't. And the guard didn't know about the car," says Billy. "I think we are safe."

They light cigarettes and smoke as the sun starts to rise.

"This is your fault, Joey. I'm really upset with you. Why did you run the wrong way? Are you crazy? You fool!" says Billy.

"I'm sorry. I couldn't see! It was dark!" says Joey.

"Never do that again!" says Billy.

"I won't. I promise," says Joey.

"You have to be more professional Joey. You have to improve. This is a serious job. If we get caught, we will go to jail for a very long time. Do you understand?"

"Sorry Billy," says Joey. He feels bad.

"Now the police are looking for us. We have to be very careful," says Billy. "Let's call Mr Sweeney and tell him we have the painting. Then, we can go straight to London and give him the painting and get the money."

"That's a good idea," says Joey.

"I'm going to call Mr Sweeney now," says Billy. "It's 6:00am, but he should be up. He always gets up early."

Billy gets out of the car and stretches. He breathes in the clear morning air and then dials Mr Sweeney's mobile phone number.

Joey closes his eyes. He hopes this can end quickly. He wants to give the painting to Mr Sweeney as soon as possible. Then, he wants to get the money and stop being an art thief. He doesn't want to do this anymore.

Billy comes back to the car. He opens the door slowly and sits down. He drops the phone on the floor.

"Billy? What's wrong? Are you OK?" asks Joey.

Billy's face is white. He cannot speak.

"Billy, what is it? What's wrong?" says Joey. "Tell me!"

"It's…it's…M..Mr… Sw..Swee…Sweeney," whispers Billy.

"What? What is it?" shouts Joey.

"Mr Sweeney is dead," whispers Billy.

"What?!" Joey looks at Billy. "Dead?! What do you mean? Do you mean…he is…he is…dead?"

"Yes. He's…he's…dead. When I called his mobile phone, his wife answered. Mr Sweeney had a heart attack at around 3:00am this morning," whispers Billy.

"3:00am?" Suddenly Joey feels very cold. "Billy, we stole the painting at around 3:00am," he says.

Billy and Joey both look at the painting. Then they look at each other.

Billy lights another cigarette.

"What are we going to do? What are we going to do?" asks Joey. He is frightened.

"I don't know!" shouts Billy. "I don't know!"

Billy is very frightened too. He wants to sell the painting, but the buyer, Mr Sweeney, is now dead. He closes his eyes and covers his face with his hands.

"Give me a few minutes to think Joey," he says.

Joey and Billy sit in silence for a few minutes. Then, suddenly, Billy sits up.

"Joey! I have an idea. There's a rich art collector in Edinburgh. I sometimes steal paintings for him. He might want to buy it. I'll call him now," says Billy.

"Good idea!" says Joey.

Billy dials the art collector's number and waits.

"He isn't answering his phone," says Billy.

"It is quite early Billy. Maybe he is sleeping," says Joey.

"Yeah, you're right. I'll try again in an hour."

Billy tries to call the art collector many times, but he doesn't answer his phone. Billy is starting to get worried. He wants to sell the painting as quickly as possible.

"I don't want to wait any longer. I know his address, and Edinburgh is not so far. It's only a few hours up the motorway. I'll drive up to Edinburgh and try to find him," says Billy.

"Can I come too?" asks Joey.

"No. You go back to the flat with the painting and wait," says Billy.

"Aren't you going to take the painting?" asks Joey.

"No, it's too dangerous. I don't trust the art collector. I want to negotiate the payment before I take the painting to him. I will take a photograph of the painting and show him the photograph to prove we have it. Then, if he wants it, we can take it up there together."

"OK," says Joey. "Be careful Billy."

"I will," says Billy. "Don't worry about me. Go back to the flat and try to get some sleep."

CHAPTER EIGHT

Joey is sitting in the living room. The painting is in the kitchen. He doesn't want to stay in the same room as the painting. He feels very frightened. Mr Sweeney died at the same time they stole it. Joey thinks the curse killed Mr Sweeney.

He lights a cigarette and looks at the clock.

"5:00pm," he says to himself. He looks at his mobile phone. "Why hasn't Billy called yet?"

Before he left, Billy said, "I'll call when I arrive in Edinburgh at around 4:00pm."

Maybe there is heavy traffic on the motorway, thinks Joey.

Joey is bored. He goes to the kitchen and makes a cup of coffee. He looks at the painting. It is rolled up, like a tube. He picks it up and unrolls it. He looks at the girl. She is smiling softly at him.

"Did you kill Mr Sweeney?" he whispers. "Did you?"

The girl looks at him from the painting. Joey's hands start to shake and sweat. He rolls the painting up again and puts it on the counter. He picks up his coffee and goes into the living room. He doesn't want to look at the painting anymore.

It is 10:00pm. Joey is very worried. Billy still hasn't called. He tries to call Billy, but his phone is switched off.

He switches the TV on. The news is starting.

"Good evening, this is the ten o clock news," says the newscaster. "Tonight, we bring you news of an accident on the A1 motorway near Edinburgh. At 3:00pm this afternoon, a large truck crashed into the back of a car. The truck driver escaped with minor injuries, but the car driver died at the scene. Police do not know his name, but they say he was a man, aged around forty years old, with brown hair. He was driving a brown car. The owner of the car was a man named Mr Sweeney. Mr Sweeney died of a heart attack last night. If you know the man, please call the police…the number is…"

Joey runs to the TV screen. "Billy! Billy! Oh no! Billy! Is that you? No!!" he screams. "Billy is dead! Oh no! Oh God, please help me! No!"

He falls to the floor and cries and cries. "Billy! Billy! Billy! You were like an older brother to me! I loved you Billy! Why! Why did you have to die? Why?!!"

Mr Sweeney is dead. Billy is dead. Joey switches the TV off. Silence fills the dark room. The window is open and a cold wind is blowing into the flat. He looks at the kitchen door.

"It's you…you killed Billy…you killed Billy," he whispers angrily. "You! The girl in the blue dress! You killed Billy!"

Joey tries to stand up, but he is too upset. His legs are shaking. He crawls on his hands and knees to the kitchen door and opens it. He crawls to the counter and tries to stand up. He looks at the picture again.

That's strange, he thinks. *She isn't smiling anymore. She looks angry and sad…her eyes look very dark…*

Joey starts to feel sick.

"I must take the painting back," he whispers. "I must take it back. If I don't take it back, she will kill me too." He sits down on the floor. "I don't want to be an art thief anymore. I don't want to do this anymore. I want a real job," he whispers to the painting. "I promise I will take you back. I will take you back to the castle. I will take you back. Please don't hurt me. Please. "

Joey lies on the floor all night and cries.

CHAPTER NINE

Joey opens his eyes. It is morning. He looks out of the window. It is raining very heavily and the clouds are heavy and grey. He remembers Billy and starts to cry again. Then, he remembers the painting and he feels very frightened.

"I have to take the painting back," he says. "But how? I don't have a car anymore."

He lights a cigarette and thinks for a few minutes.

The castle is about ten miles away. I can walk, or maybe there is a bus. Or I could get a taxi, he thinks.

He gets up and walks over to the window. The rain is getting heavier. It is hitting the window very hard.

I can't walk in this weather. The painting will get wet, he thinks.

He looks down to the road. There is a bus stop outside the flat.

I can get the bus into the city centre, and then find a bus to the castle, he thinks. *But, how can I take the painting into the castle? There will be many security guards and more security cameras now. Someone will see me. What would Billy do? What would Billy do if he was here with me?*

He closes his eyes and thinks about Billy.

"Billy! What should I do? Billy! Help me please!" he cries. "Billy! Where are you? Please help me!"

Then, he hears Billy's voice in his head.

"Joey! Post it! And stop crying like a baby, you fool!"

He opens his eyes.

Yes! That's a great idea! I can post it! Yes! I can buy a big envelope, and send it by post to the castle! Yes! Nothing bad will happen to me in the post office.

Then, I can get the train back to London. Then everything will be finished.

Joey looks out of the window. He looks up at the grey sky.

"Thank you Billy," he whispers.

But what will I do in London? I have no business partner. Billy was my partner and friend. Now, I have no one…no job…no money…

He looks at the clock. It is 9:00am.

I will think about that later. Now, I have to send the painting, he thinks.

He puts his coat on and goes into the kitchen. He picks up the painting.

"I'm taking you to the post office and then I'm sending you home, OK?" he says to the painting. "Then, please forget about me."

He puts the painting under his coat and leaves the apartment.

Joey walks out into the rain. He is worried about the curse. Will he be safe? The bus stop is just across the road. He looks down the road and sees a bus. The road is very busy, so he cannot cross the road yet. The bus is getting closer.

It is still raining heavily, and the rain is falling down his coat. If he doesn't catch the bus, he will have to wait for the next bus. The painting will get very wet. He decides to run across the road. He steps out into the road very carefully and starts running. The bus is getting closer. The road is very wet and slippery.

He gets to the other side of the road, and then suddenly his foot slips and he falls to the ground!

He looks up and sees the bus coming towards him!

"No! No! The curse! It's the curse! The painting! Oh no! Don't kill me!" he shouts. "Don't kill me! I'm sorry!"

He hears people shouting at him. They are telling him to move, but he cannot move. His ankle is broken. He hears the brakes of the bus, as the driver tries to stop. He hears a woman screaming. He closes his eyes and he sees the girl in the painting. She is laughing. He can hear her laughter.

Then he feels something hard and cold hit his head. Then, everything goes black.

CHAPTER TEN

Joey opens his eyes. The light is very bright. He sees a man sitting next to his bed.

"Where am I?" he asks the man.

"You are in hospital," says the man.

"Hospital? Why?" asks Joey. He is confused. "And, who are you?"

"I am a police officer," says the man.

"A police officer?" asks Joey. "Why are you here?"

"When the bus hit you, someone called the police and an ambulance. When we arrived, you were unconscious. People said, 'He was screaming about a painting and a curse.' We opened your coat and we found the painting. We arrested you. When you are better, we are going to take you to the police station," says the policeman.

Joey closes his eyes again. Then, he remembers...the painting...Billy...the bus...

Oh no! I have been caught! he thinks.

He looks at the policeman. "Where is the painting?" he whispers.

"We are taking it back to the castle. It has a little damage, but not too much," says the policeman.

"And what about me?" asks Joey.

"You are going to jail for a long time," says the policeman. "A very long time."

Joey lies back and closes his eyes. *My mother will be so disappointed! She thinks I work in a bank! I hope this is a dream,* he thinks. *I hope this is a dream.*

"I didn't want to steal the painting. I really didn't," says Joey.

"Tell that to the judge and the court!" says the police officer.

CHAPTER ELEVEN

Lord and Lady Boglow stand in the girl's room in the castle. They are watching their staff put the painting back on the wall. The painting was damaged a little, but an art specialist repaired it.

"Welcome home," says Lord Boglow VI to the painting.

"We have to be more careful. Even with the curse, some people will try and steal it," says Lady Boglow.

"Well, this is the fifth time, and this time too, one thief was killed on the motorway, and another was hit by a bus. And the buyer of the painting died, too. So, I don't think anyone will try to steal it again," says Lord Boglow VI. "And we have more security cameras now, and an alarm on the window."

"I hope you are right," says Lady Boglow. Then, she moves closer to the painting.

"Look…that's strange," she says.

"What is it?" asks Lord Boglow VI.

"There is something different about the painting." Lady Boglow looks very closely at it.

"What is different?" asks the lord.

The lady thinks for a moment.

"Look at her face. Her face is different. Her smile…yes, her smile!" says the lady. "Before, her smile was a gentle smile. But now, her smile looks very big!"

Lord Boglow VI looks more closely. Then he smiles.

"Yes, I think you are right!" he says in surprise. "She does look very happy."

They walk out of the room and close the door.
On the wall, the girl in the blue dress smiles. She is home again.

THANK YOU

Thank you for reading The Curse. (Word count: 7,623) We hope you enjoyed it.

There are quizzes about this book on our free study site I Talk You Talk Press EXTRA. http://italk-youtalk.com

If you would like to read more graded readers, please visit our website http://www.italkyoutalk.com

Other Level 3 graded readers include
A Dangerous Weekend
A Holiday to Remember
Akiko and Amy Part 1
Akiko and Amy Part 2
Akiko and Amy Part 3
Be My Valentine
Different Seas
Enjoy Your Business Trip
Enjoy Your Homestay
I Need a Friend
Old Jack's Ghost Stories from England (1)
Old Jack's Ghost Stories from England (2)
Old Jack's Ghost Stories from Ireland
Old Jack's Ghost Stories from Japan
Old Jack's Ghost Stories from Scotland

Old Jack's Ghost Stories from Wales
Party Time!
Stories for Christmas
Together Again
Who is Holly?

ABOUT THE AUTHOR

I Talk You Talk Press is a Japan-based publisher of language textbooks, graded readers and language learning/teaching resources.

Our team is made up of highly experienced language teachers and translators, who have all studied at least one additional language to an advanced level.

This experience enables us to design our materials from the perspective of both the teacher and the learner. We consult with both teachers and language learners when designing our textbooks and graded readers, and test our materials extensively in the classroom before publication.

We are a fast-growing press, and currently publish graded readers for learners of English. We publish new graded readers monthly.

www.ingramcontent.com/pod-product-compliance
Lightning Source LLC
Chambersburg PA
CBHW022349040426
42449CB00006B/796